I0440839

A Whippersnapper's Snapshot of AWAKENING
and the water is blue

by
Sinnbad Kaashin

email: sinnbadkaashin@gmail.com

Table of Content

Introduction   i

Chapter 1   THE FLOOR OF TIME   1

Chapter 2   THE BARKING ZEBRA   10

Chapter 3   DOG LOVERS   21

Chapter 4   FIGHT OR FLIGHT   28

Chapter 5   THE TREE OF PAIN   35

Chapter 6   THE MISSING COMB   43

Chapter 7   CRYING FOR THE VISA   50

Chapter 8   THE MOSQUITO BITES   57

Chapter 9   IT DEPENDS   65

Introduction

This book, as the its name suggests, is a book of experiments not conducted in a controlled environment, but in a live environment where the uncertainty of the outcome is always certain. I call such an environment, life. Most experiences are taken from the lives of the people with whom I have had the opportunity to share my own. Extensive care has been taken to not temper with the original experiences. It was necessary to do so because it was the only way to make you go to the depth of the problems that these experiences bring out for us to solve. And if not to solve, then at least learn something useful out of those experiences.

The name of the book was a challenge, and after a deep discussion with my wife, I named it the way she suggested. My choice was very simple. I wanted to name it as, 'The Color of Water is Blue.' And my wife said it sounded more like a romantic fiction novel. Well, I kept the name she told me after reading it, but I kept mine too. You will find the reason why I named it, 'and the water is blue,' very interesting.

I was trying to solve the problem of naming this book, while jogging on a street in Mumbai on a hot summer evening. I crossed a vegetable vendor's trolley. There on the trolley, I saw potatoes that looked very appealing to me. I do not get attracted to potatoes normally, but I guess it was due to the fact that to make them appealing, the vendor had sprinkled water all over them. Not only the potatoes, but all the vegetables on his small shop on the wheels were wet. Now, why would some potatoes that are sprinkled with water attract a guy who is running in his shorts and vests. And that too when there are beautiful people on the street, whose DNA have evolved to have more attraction coding than in that of a potato's. I guess I know the reason. I was on my Navratri fasts during that time. Not only a fast for celibacy, but also for food. I was not only hungry, but as I was running on empty stomach, my animal instincts must have awakened upon the view of a lot of fresh wet potatoes. Incidentally, I had bought a few potatoes last night, but they were not wet when I bought them. And my dry potatoes were the first thought that ran in my head when I saw those wet, fleshy and mind-blowing potatoes. If I hadn't had bought those dry potatoes that were lying in my kitchen, I would have surely bought some for me from that very vendor. Anyhow, I reminded myself that I was not an animal, if only social, and I controlled my urge to go back home, wet my potatoes, and see if they looked the same as the vendor's potatoes did. Keeping that thought alive, I continued my run. As soon as I got back home, I wetted my goddam potatoes. And say what? Remarkably, after about fifteen minutes lying in the water, they looked better than the vendor's potatoes.

So, the deserts are red and the forests are green, but who can argue that the water isn't blue. Deserts are dry of water. Forests are full of water. My potatoes were mine, but they were a desert without water. The vendor's potatoes were full of water, but they were not mine. There will always be something that will lack one or two major ingredients. And sometimes nothing will be appealing on its own, until we do something about it. And that is the theme of this book. I cannot prove that water is blue, but if any color of water is true, it is blue.

Considering the desert and forest theory, and considering that RBG stands for Red, Blue and Green, then Red is for desert and Green is for the forest, where the water is then surely blue for me. Molecules of water scatter light in the sky that make it look blue. I don't give a damn to what anyone say, I say the water is blue. Well, do not worry, this book is in no way an attempt to prove anything. The glory of proof lives shorter than a lightening.

Anyhow, none of that shit impressed my wife, and she named the book as you know it now. If you are married, and if you manage to remain smart, you will always find it good to put your titles in italics and small, while I suggest you put your wife's in capital and bold.

Though it is a short piece of work, the effort to bring some weird but important aspects of life on paper, or maybe on your tablets, took a good amount of time. The secret to anything is time.

At many places I have discussed about people suffering from diseases and participating in some activities that may seem weird or unspeakable of. To explain some ideas, I have used examples of people who have suffered from cancer and were strong enough to come out of it. I want to clarify that I didn't have cancer, but yes, I have had a benign tumor in my parotid gland. I am happy to tell you that it was removed along with my lower left globe of parotid gland itself. The doctor who operated me is the most confident and most positive human being I had ever encountered in an operation theatre at eight o'clock in the morning. He calmly walked to me and said, "You are brave, and everything will be fine." I thank him for those words, because those were the last words I heard, before spending a good nine hours in the world of general anesthesia. I thank God almighty for giving me that tumor and then coming in the form of that doctor to remove it. I am grateful to have gone through that phase of my life. It taught me a very good lesson. I learnt that no matter who you are, where you are and what you are, there will be times when things will happen to you that you will not be able to solve on your own. You will need people around you in such times. If you will trust in God, He will walk with you by becoming those people through those dark moments. He will show you the light when your own lamp will be out of fuel. Well, God has a lot of work to do other than that too, so do not also completely rely on Him. Because, when you will be out in light. He will want you to become his messenger and show light to others in need.

Unlike other self-help books this isn't a self-help book alone. Sometimes while reading it you might be needing some exterior help too. Do not mind asking for it. Extensive care has been taken to not use curse words, but wherever they were necessary they are appropriately used. I do not have any shame in using such words because they came out impromptu. They came when I was filled with emotions and I did not edit them as you will find that they are not a part of the larger script.

After long and thorough examination of the way this book has been put together, I believe it will be a task for you to read it. Do not bother reading it in one go, as it will not happen anyway. Both the extent and the depth this book to the human psyche are reachable. And since you have already picked it for reading it in your own leisure time, I believe you will spend that unit of time in leisure. Although, while you will read further you will realize that most of the content here was initially out of the scope of this book, but out of the shear necessity those content made a seat in here. You can assume that the party you are going to attend in this book will be full of guests who were passing by the street while the party was on. Somehow most of them liked the sound of the music and stayed sometime longer in here. I believe that to express fully a writer should be able to risk spanning into areas that are less ventured into traditionally by many. Mostly, out fear of losing the interest of the reader. This is a very valid reason, of course. But to an extent this is confined to the topics that are limited. Like, fishing. Fishing is a topic where one will not discuss the Great Pyramids.

There are nine divisions that have been made into as chapters. Before starting, I asked myself, why do they have the paragraphs or the chapters? Having all the three meals in one go is never advisable. Anyhow, that is how we humans have evolved. Taking one bite at a time, of one course at a time, of a day at a time. If the doctor asks us to eat seven apples in a week, he surely means an apple a day. Dear Sinnbad cannot eat all the seven on a single Sunday in one go. That is the reason why I was forced to divide my work first into chapters and then into paragraphs. And when I fragmented it, it converted from what was just a random scribble on a paper into a book that made sense.

So, I converted my big scribble into a decent looking book. I believe that in every book the paragraphs are the cities, the chapters are the states, and the book is a country in itself. And managing a country is far easier when there are ministers of states and mayors in the cities.

Every chapter begins with parts that will tell the first-hand experience of the incident that I went through in a matter of just a few seconds. And few here actually means few. If the reader wants to know what happened in that incident, I can tell you right here and now what it was. And I am not in any way trying to dupe you or myself by giving you the spoiler or by giving away my book in one sentence. Here is what really happened:

I just woke up, I found myself weeping and then, I smiled. Yes, this is all that this book is about. Usually when I tell people this, they ask me if I had a bad dream, or did I hurt myself by sleeping in some weird posture? To that I say this...

Chapter 1

The FLOOR of TIME

I woke up, if at all I did, after what I call a very brief nap. There was a deep sadness all around me and strangely, I could smell that sadness in the air. The olfactory function of our brain relates to the sense of smell. While it is used to smell anything and everything, its function is directly related to our memories. Memories, obviously of the past, because I have never met a person who has the memories of the future.

In most mammals and insects, it is a question of life and death when it comes down to olfactory function. The herbivores in the jungles depend on their sense of smell to keep themselves aware of the dangers around them. The olfactory function long thought to be obsolete in us the humans, the new studies have found that it is very closely related to our memory. Since our emotions are memory oriented, it is not a wonder when you suddenly get a surge in your joy and in your overall happiness, when after a mild rain you get the first gush of the petrichor. Ever imagined why we are repulsed to the foul-smelling stale food, or a carcass? Well, the harmful effects of involving ourselves with such things are deeply coded in our very DNA. Evolution has carefully stored every experience, good or bad, that our ancestors have gone through over a course of millions of years. And by ancestors, I do not mean only us the humans, or the great apes. I mean the very fauna itself. This recorded history in our DNA, we call it memory, is reactivated upon encountering foul-smell. Be it a child, a grown-up, someone in this part of the world or that, our response is always the same.

Sadness, as for me, seemed to have had flung opened the forbidden gates of my memory. It was like it had walked right up to the present me through the corridor of my warped past. Contrary to my belief that there can be no way of burrowing through this cemented corridor of time, that gets frozen the moment it happens, it was standing through and through wide open in front of me; a hallway of my past shining right through my soul. I could see the light coming from the other end of the corridor. It was like I was sitting on the floor that led back to my childhood. And the only thing I needed to do was to get up and start walking back to my own self. And that's exactly what I did.

This was the very beginning of a very old affair with its direction turning the other way around. An affair with time. What went around from me had finally found its way back to me. Like sound echoing without loss, it was a voyage to be taken but, on the ship that we all think moves only in one direction; forward. Well, I cannot claim that I know, but yes, I do believe that time can move in any direction it pleases. It moves wherever it wants to. When does it do that? Oh, that is a question that it doesn't get bothered about. Because when you are on a ship that is time itself, there is no hurry, no delay. Everything happens just in time. Anyhow, time here too isn't in the scope of this short book. Just like my dog, time too will require a separate book altogether.

Time, like everything else around me, had made itself comfortable somewhere in that clock at that late morning hour. In times of ordinary flow of life, it becomes difficult to be comfortable with time. Time seems so humble and remains a point of reference to most of us. And when we realize that there is nowhere else that we can run from here, the extraordinary happens. We see that time has paused for a moment. During a loss, a tragedy, natural or man-made disaster, or in some other insidious uninvited event, there is a point where almost everything seizes to make sense. It is a paradox. Even the clinical psychologists approve of the fact that a patient, suffering from cancer, turns into someone so immensely positive, even after he is made known the exact reason and time he is going to die. Miraculously, many of those patients cure themselves of the disease. Take themselves out of such deep traumatic circumstances. How do you think that becomes possible? When, in times like these, we find ourselves fighting with our invisible selves to get up from the couch and take a brisk walk in the evening, and that too while we are perfectly healthy, how do these degenerated, hopeless beings gather the encouragement or motivation to run marathons, climb mountains and do wonders that we all very healthy will only watch others doing on the television from the same couch? May be the so-called life, that was running smoothly, suddenly turns into a real life for such people. Another explanation is that time, that for most remains a commodity of infinite abundance, becomes scarce for such people. Well, I do not want to bore you with this detail of what happens in those times when you can see your grave in some countable distance.

But just like them for me, a pause button over the time had appeared out from nowhere and clicked itself into action. The action that let me see time as it was. And not as a tamer with a hunter or just a hand on the dial, or that blinking colon on that digital watch. It suddenly became something very real. I know you cannot touch time, but you can touch yourself right now and feel yourself. Well, you are a product of every event happening exactly at the right time and in the right place. Well, how about your parents decided to not sleep together, the night they did nine months before you came out in this world? You would have been someone who was watching a movie, instead of this book right now. There can be all sort of possibilities. The possibility of being the other gender, in some different city, or a very different profession. Well, this is what we have name, probability. Now, according to the American Cancer Society, the probability of encountering cancer in one's life is almost 0.4 in males. It translates to that almost forty percent of the males are going to have cancer somewhere or the other in the course of their lifetimes. Well, it is what the statistics say.

So, being in that state was as if the greatest truth has revealed itself. Like, when the child starts walking, or speaking, it is a moment of wonder and awe for the parents. They react in a way, as if their ward is the first one to walk on the planet. But these are the events that force us to pause and take a moment of appreciation. The moment, that we stopped taking for own self somewhere in the process of growing smarter and better human beings, is once again offered by the God almighty. Earlier, before this event – miraculously designed only for me – that I am glad of – there was this not-very-me, that kept pushing me towards everything that the very-me didn't want to be pushed towards. Suddenly, that not-very-me took a turn and started walking away from the very-me.

The knowledge of finite time is by far the only feeling that somehow validates the existence of death. One might come to near vague experience of death while attending a funeral, but we cannot experience it exclusively for ourselves in those moments. This is because, funerals are inherently devoted to the soul that has departed for the heavens than to those who attend it. When I first attended a funeral, I remember the fear I underwent, but the behavior of the primates who were present was extremely comforting. In most funerals the attendees predominantly assume a role that of a mourner. This behavior of expressing grief on someone's death is not limited to us humans. It has been found that some species of monkeys and other distant primates too grieve their dead ones. The purpose and the beginning of mourning is too deeply engraved in our being and may be that is the reason death has been chosen as an example here.

To know that someone is going to die or that someone is dead triggers a feeling of grief, but that grief is defined by the kind of relationship we have with the deceased or the diseased. This grief cannot be translated into a very strong feeling unless that someone is our kith and kin or a very close loved one. But the person who himself is the victim as well as the mourner, that is a person who comes to the knowing that some sort of ailment has taken over him and that he is going to die, experiences a peculiar conundrum between life and death. There arises a very big question in one's mind. To plainly live or to live while thinking of dying every step of the way? This problem is experienced by every soldier during war, every convict on a death row, every stuntman in action, every sailor on a voyage and every patient who has been refused any treatment for his fatal ailment. The knowledge that others can only do so much for his state of being, keeps him coming back to himself. A lady experiencing labor pain for the first time can suitably be put in that position. Although a woman gives birth to a human being, her own state in particular is as delicate as that of the little guest. Not every woman who gives birth to a child survives. Not every soldier who goes to war returns home. Not every man that walks on this planet today, will be walking here a year later. But the myth is we think that being unbeknownst to the impending death gives us the liberty to enjoy every moment of our lives happily.

The concoction, of the unbearable pain and the fear of slipping in to the darkness forever, creates a fire within us. This fire illuminates a very dark path ahead that has no sign-boards, no physical representation of any kind anywhere and is analogous to nothing to the human knowledge. If I can be bold enough to say, 'the knowledge of infinite books cannot equate the knowledge of the finite time.' The knowledge, that the time here on this planet is finite, makes the expenditure of the same, with acute measure, of necessity. The rationing of time has been discussed in the bible. In Psalm 90:12 it says, "Teach us to number our days, that we may gain a heart of wisdom."

In the nineties the Mahabharata was televised so much that, its beginning has got stuck in my mind. It used to start with a very echoed manly voice saying, "Main samaya hoon…." That translates to, "I am time…." The human spirit has been always curious about the time itself. But in the process of growing in some areas of life, this curiosity diminishes and when not nurtured enough, gets lost in the sand of time.

Well, the knowledge of finite time isn't a bad thing after all. In some time, the mind gets tired of the information of the impending death. The good thing is in such times of adversity, the brain and the whole biome in our intestine change shapes and chemistry to drive us through it. The realization, of life being a precious commodity and not just being any random gift out of a million that everyone alive has been awarded with, becomes very powerful. First of all, such information is very scarcely distributed among pupils because it is only seen relevant to those who undergo through tough times in life. Such philosophical ideas are of little to no use in a corporation where every single person is running after making their lives better and better. Whereas, in the course of making it better, we have a feeling of living somewhere outside of it. This is known as the Construction Syndrome.

Imagine you are building a home. Also, you have nowhere else to live other than either in a motel, your car, or if you are lucky maybe at your workplace. This kind of lifestyle is discouraged in the society. Not because it is bad, but because it is difficult. People in difficult times take drastic steps to change their situations by first changing their attitude toward the situation. Since living out on the bare minimum, including time, is so very tough, crossing such situations becomes a victory in itself. This destructive state is a very peculiar kind of constructive stage of life. It forces one to focus on something so strongly that other seemingly important issues seem to slide away for that short period of time.

Chapter 2

BARKING ZEBRA

To clearly tell what it was, whether a proper nap or a half-nap-half-awake thing has remained a quandary to this very day. And with a guy like me, it shall remain the same until I take up that herculean task of getting down to the deepest corners of my brain to fish out that perfect instant. The instant that I had lost in time. Sometimes, recalling a thought becomes one draining task for me. And it is all the more irksome if you wake up to one big headache. A headache about which you know only one thing, that you don't know nothing about it. Well, I once spent a solid two hundred and fifty kilometers in distance and six and a half hours in time consistently recalling one very unimportant thought that just came and went by, like a fart. What made things worse was that during those two hundred and fifty kilometers and six and a half hours, I knew the thought that I had lost in my brain was extremely unimportant. Having this fact at hand, I cared not to involve myself in any remotely seeming important topic with the two of my good friends I was travelling with. They say the biggest battle is fought between your ears. Well, one has to start practicing somewhere. Though that fart like thought must have been ahead of the Voyager by now and I guess it will reflect back to me once it touches the corner of the Universe.

I love this goddam language. You can write whatever you want and let read whatever they do. I tell you if Pfizer had any momentary effect at all on the tool, it still would have got beaten by this goddam language alone. My grandfather. Yes, I had one. And he had a huge respect for both, the language and the men who brought it to us here in India. The English. Yeah! That's the fucking point. The language and the natives of this goddam language are both named, English. I mean, it's nothing new. Many do. Like, Chinese, Japanese, Russian, Mexican, Punjabi, or a few more, like almost all of them, save for just Hindi, Urdu, and a few more. You will never see an Urdu guy walking down the street. He may talk there in Urdu, but he won't walk down the goddam street. But you can always find someone who is English, who is walking down the same street, with another someone who is again English sitting by the side on the same goddam street and they both will smile at each other and say just anything whatsoever in the goddam English.

My grandfather was in the Indian Air Force, where even the mutes can communicate only in English. Imagine that you are on an airstrip of any of the Indian Air Force wings anywhere in India, and you want to fucking fly a Mirage, or the MIG for the fuck sake. And if you will ask them this little favor, like getting your hands on the keys to that goddam fighter jet, you may want to ask them in fucking English. That may not be a sure shot way to make them handover the keys to the fucking jet to you, but if you still have your balls orbiting your ass, you bet, it will fucking impress those rascals. One more reason that I believe my grandfather loved the language was that he was born way before the so-called independence we received. Well, we are independent now, but of what, I don't know. And that receiving dropped in with a hell lot of a baggage. The irony that we live in here with is that the baggage contained a few very interesting things. One of them is cricket, the game. Yeah? Isn't it a sport? Why call it a game? Well, ask the International Olympic Committee. They haven't officially introduced this game to their list of games in the Olympics. Well, we don't give a damn about it. We have just become a cricket nation and what's hilarious is that we play it far better than the English themselves. There are fifty-three well-lit cricket grounds in India compared to twenty-two in the United Kingdom, less than half. This isn't a mushrooming of grounds out of shear love for the game. Neither it is because we have to compete with other nations. The reason for embracing this game so hard by this nation has very different roots and are in a way valid too. The game, I emphasize, is not a sport. In test the crew, the team, members can go on for five to seven long days, bowling and batting one another. A total of around four-hundred-and-fifty overs are bowled in a typical test match. In ODI, abbreviation for One Day International, they ball a total of hundred overs. Seeing the growing impatience among the new generation, they have come up with a solution known as twenty-twenty. As the name suggests this very short version of game, still not a sport, consists of forty overs.

Invented by some British kids for their entertainment, the game has reached all the British colonies and is now second most spectator game after soccer. Well, the popularity of the game in India is due to the rest period between every over. The bowler changes, the batsmen go and talk stuff, discuss the pace and shit in that time. Well, what do the TV guys do? They don't show all that boring stuff to us. We don't want to see two batsmen chatting or scratching their crotches with their mickey-mouse gloves. The TV guys slide in a few very attractive commercials while we eagerly wait for the next over to begin. If you get time to listen to the radio commentary of a match, you will notice even the fours and sixes are commercialized over there. Whenever a guy hits a four or a six, they will play a short recorded commercial, "And this was BSNL six…." Well, I am not against the game, but I don't even like it. The thing is that the popularity of the game is because of its pattern and that it has suited the companies to pay for their commercials.

This micro-commercial thing is now possible with other sports too, but every seed that plants itself in the shadow of a bigger one, shall perish even before it germinates.

Well, that that getting born before the English, who imaginarily freed us from something, made him, my grandfather, interact with quite a lot of white guys. So, he could fucking walk the talk and give a couple of Indian guys jitters down their goddam spines with it. Even though he was way down in the eighties when he lived with me in my room, he had this fire for the words he could kill a mammoth with.

I don't give a fuck to the proper usage of the goddam language. To my happiness, my grandfather had already freed me from it. Like I cannot and will never kill my time thinking whether it is, "...in his late eighties...," or, "...way down in the eighties...." The fact is that, since I was a kid, I had imagined the numbers to be in their primitive rows. I got no time to arrange them again to something else. I like them there. I just love the way it is, like it was. Like from one to ten is one row, eleven to twenty another, and so on. But the ones, like all of them starting from one, eleven, twenty-one, and so on, they are all on the top. Then you start climbing down the rows. And when you finish with one row, you pop out from the top of the next one in an instant. It is like Super Mario. Mathematicians saved us from climbing up the fucking infinity ladder. With the numbers in rows you are always somewhere or the other, but you just have to climb down to move ahead in counting. Well, for clock it is different. It comes down twice and climbs up twice a day. Poor thing. I just feel nauseated with this thought in my head.

So, my grandfather was way down in the eighties row, when he used to live with me, in my room. Like somewhere near that eight or that nine. And I tell you, it's no joke, that I cannot stand the sight of any living or dead person in my fucking room, even for a second, or a femtosecond, for that matter. But with him, my grandfather, it was different. I guess, the only person with whom I can be alive and happy at the same time, and that too in my room, it was him, my grandfather. Yeah, sadly he is no more, but I am happy for him, that he could get his ticket up there. Well, I can stand his ghost too, if that be the case. I so wish it to be like that. I do miss him. You know why? Because he fucking respected almost everything he did, or I did, or whosoever did what on this goddam planet. He gave an ear to the talk, an eye to the sight, a nose to the air and a hand to whatever he felt needed his care. I see people who do not respect shit, all the time. I mean they don't give a fuck to what in the hell goes around. I mean, let alone the goddam planet, they don't give a fuck to what happens to themselves. They make me sick to my smallest intestine. Though, they don't. That's just a metaphor that I made up. And I don't think there's even small intestine, the fucking medical guys, they already are of no use. I just don't like the metaphors that are already used up. Like, used up to their last fucking drop of sanity. So, I spend time building my own. But

I tell you it is fucking amazing to see that those fuckers are so immune to life. Not the medical fuckers. The fuckers who don't give a fuck to the right things in life. That doesn't piss me off, though. I am immune to getting pissed off. Whatever, the point is I don't like being in my room with somebody who doesn't give a fuck to at least one goddam thing that can be of interest. Of course, of my interest. Like anything. I say, may be even something immortal. Like I give a fuck all the time to almost anything. For example, I give fuck to the fucking astronomy. I really like it up there. There, in the midst of an ongoing supernova. Somewhere where the nearest galaxy is some millions of light years away. Somewhere in another solar system that is not bigger than my goddam room. Or somewhere in the anus of a black-hole itself. No! I am not a pervert. I truly believe, I am a fucking believer. Believe me you. Hold on! Who started this phrase? There may be something wrong with the ways I have been brought up. I don't know, but it becomes so goddam difficult for me to stand a phrase so artificial. I can murder the goddam believer who fucking believes me you. And I can do it, believe me you. Anyway, I believe the black-holes are really the holes. The ass-holes of the Universe itself. You know, the real spinster fitted ass-holes. The cosmic dance and the black-holes. I really enjoy that stuff.

So, I like it solo. Like all alone. And it becomes a nightmare for me to have some guy coming up to my room to stay over for a night or a couple. I do not instantly kill him, just that I get too busy with my own fucking thing. I secretly peep through between my body and my arms, to see if that kills him. I don't do anything in particular, just pretend to be very fucking busy. So busy that a right crowd will appoint me the fucking president of some hotshot country without a vote. See the thing is that almost always it is like, I do not do anything. I just, am. Truly, what in the heaven can you do? "Oh! I do the work man!" Really? Is that all, you were born to fucking do? Know that nothing can be finished once started. I have worked on my own and for other bastards as well, but really it made no difference. Like, when I joined my first office, I thought the work will sum up in a week or two, but guess what? It did not. It is not going to stop anytime ever. This thing, this shit we think we DO, is never going to end. So, any participation whatsoever is just a fucking participation. Groucho Marx said, "I refuse to join any club that have me as a member." He dismissed the idea of mere participation. It's a mess when we start doing something just for the sake of doing it. There is so much that can be done by not doing it. I just lie on my bed, jerk off at times, watch the goddam tv switch off when it is on. Just that. I pretend that I work all the time, but truly, I am the laziest mammal ever born on the chest of the mother nature. The sloth puts up a great freaking show about being slow and all. Though, it too has its own limitations, I tell you. But me? Man, I can slow down so much that you can see the Sun coming up and going down like a bullet, but you won't see me going in to the bed or coming out of it ever. My mom, she was twenty when I slowly came into this world. Now, she is fifty, and I tell you in these thirty years she has never seen me either going to the bed or coming out of it.

Sometimes if the guy, the one in my room, doesn't give a fuck to something he should, makes the nightmare grow. So, if he doesn't give a fuck to why or what in the hell, I am busy with, that just makes me go fucking Zodiac. Well, all you can do is, pretend. Just fucking pretend that you are busy with something. While, he may just keep on barking like a fucking zebra. You know zebras? They are the most unwanted animals on the planet. They are the worst nightmare for all the wildlife, including me. I cannot fucking stand their sight. First, they fucking pretend and try get along as if they are the fucking horses. After that they grow those controversial white stripes on their fucking black skin. I am not a racist, but I just can't take my focus off those stripes. Who knows if they are white stripes on a black skin or black stripes on a white skin? Yeah, the stripes. Almost like the ones we have on the roads, the ones we co-incidentally call zebra-crossings. And with these embezzled stripes, they have been puzzling the blacks and the whites, together, all along. I tell you if something is diplomatic in the animal kingdom, it's the zebras' stripes. And with these stripes, they come mingled up in the party of the wildebeests as if they are fucking tigers. Worst of all the miseries these monsters have managed to knit in the peaceful Savannahs is that, they fucking bark! For the fuck sake, please! This animal beats the fucking Unicorn, I tell you. I really love the horse, the tiger, and the dog for all the goddam reasons these mighty animals have to offer in their own right. No offence to these holy creatures. But, if you think you can have them all in one at once, that's something again very nauseating. It is so fucking hard to take that all in at once. I am sure, the lions must have been feeding on the grass before this fucking creature landed, I don't know from where. Maybe from the black-hole itself. And it really must have pissed the fucking lions off and finally they broke their vows to remain herbivores and ate the zebra. Who in the hell isn't pissed off by this animal? Is that even an animal? I really am immune to getting pissed off, but the zebra opened my list of exceptions here. I really give a fuck to the mother nature and the children she has given birth to, but zebra? I mean the name itself is too fucking down the alphabet. And the guy, the guy in my room, who never was there in the first place, and I am alive just to make sure that he will never be, looks at me like a fucking zebra. Leave anything that you are doing right now, except reading this book, and imagine. Just imagine a fucking zebra in your room. And now? Now imagine him barking. Fuck! I am done with the zebras and with the guy who gives a fuck to what the goddam animal wants to be. Just decide man! Just decide what you want to be.

Chapter 3

DOG LOVERS

So, I had this pain in my head, and I don't mean the headache. But to tell what it was with confirmation, is impossible. Ache is I guess the smaller version of pain. Like pain is hot, and ache is I guess only lukewarm. Though in my case the intensity of the pain was so high that I could hardly open my goddam eyes. I usually do not bother myself with an aspirin, with these stupid headaches around, but this made me think otherwise. I didn't know why it was happening to me. Reason wasn't a thing to find in that situation. So, I didn't. In fact, the time was so short that even the thought of finding it wasn't there. It could have been because of any goddam reason. I'll not blame the zebra, he wasn't there. "Maybe, it was just because of the pot I had smoked last night," I could hear myself murmuring. So, I had had my morning tea, had freshened up, and had jerked off with gusto. That last one, the jerking off part, was probably the only reason, I must have taken a nap in that late morning hour. I cannot be sure about the reason, and also exactly when and why did I lay down on my bed is missing in my working memory. I remember when I woke up my legs were dangling down the bed. They touched the floor, as my bed is almost about to sink into the floor, but still I will say they were dangling. My hands were already thrown back way beyond than they must have ever gone before. So much back that if I had to shave my own back, the only thing I would have needed was a razor. But what I remember and what I want to remember and will take with me to my grave is that it was eleven-ish when I woke up. Quite an info to make peace with in your death bed, right? That's nothing. I know people getting by with even lesser. I heard about a guy, who before dying told his wife that he cheated on her. Well, the bastard could have earned a ticket to heaven, if he had anything less stinking to tell his poor lady. Anything maybe, like anything really. Say how about you tell someone a joke before you leave for the heavens. You put a fucking smile on someone's face before the final leave. But no, people want to just clear there shit out. Even when that shit is going to hit someone hard. They do shitty things before they die, all the time. But I say he was a lucky man, though. He could think of adultery even in the death bed. I mean ordinary guy like me will die of the fear of dying itself before I will die. And he? He managed to think of all the fun he managed to collect in his lavish life and tell that all to his mommy. Well, the fucker was even luckier. He fucking died before the lady even started telling her own truth. Lucky bastard, I tell you. I pity the lady that she knew more than him, but I admire his impeccable timing too. He could manage to blurt out all he could and fucking leave without listening to her. You see? It is fucking beneficial to have as little information on hand as one can have, in this lifetime. Michael Scofield in Prison Break says, "The less you know, the better you are." And, I stopped watching the series altogether, immediately after that. Sometimes, I respect what these people have to say in the daily soaps. So, when we humans began our journey toward the light, we assumed to know more and more. But, as the light got stronger and stronger, we wanted to know less and less. It says in the bible, that blessed are those who haven't seen and have yet believed.

My immediate neighbor had a dog he brought home in its adulthood. People do things like these all the time. They bring home grown up dogs and think that they will train the hell out of them. Anyhow this dog was pretty well-trained already. Guess what? It was a Yellow Retriever Labrador. Who in the hell needs to train this one? All in correct place, but I still couldn't digest the fact that my neighbor had brought a full-grown dog to his place and always pretended that it was his dog. Well, I found something was not right with the dog. It had this whistling sound in its every bark. And it is unusual for a Labrador to bark a billion times in a day, or the whole night for that matter. You must be thinking that how in the hell I know so much about Labradors. Well, I am not a vet, I too lived with a Labrador who was about four-weeks-old when I brought him home. I was not a very great master. But my dog was the greatest dog ever. And so was my neighbor's. I won't talk about my dog here much, because he deserves a complete biopic. After all, I named him Hachi. And yes, he lived up to his name.

So, this dog, my neighbor's dog, had some difficulty in breathing as well as barking. It had a visible limp walk because of the breathing, probably. And this dog was soon sent back to from where it was brought. For this I have a theory that I concocted for myself. I believe, that every dog is a reflection of its master. So, whenever I see a man or a woman strolling a dog, I immediately come to know whether it is the master and the dog on the stroll or someone else is doing the master a favor. My dog was a total complete me. And you might think that this is impossible. Yeah, it is for those who live by the book, but for those who want to know something that the nature always wants to tell us in some or the other subtle ways, it can be of interest to them.

Next time you run in a duo, a dog and the stroller, try and figure out if that stroller is the master. This might sound weird, but it is true. What you will see is that the dog looks exactly the same as its master. Now you must be crazy if you think that their faces match. But they will. You will not be able to tell how they match, but they will match. Look closer, whatever the breed of the dog, the earlier the dog started growing with the master, the stronger the reflection will be. Now this doesn't end to just the physical reflections. It also includes everything else. The behavior, the barking, the swiftness, the slowness, and just about everything.

For example, dogs raised by violent people tend to show violence as their primary behavior, whereas dogs raised by stupid people tend to show stupidity as their primary behavior. Take for example, you bring home a puppy and you start beating it up from the day one. You stick to the routine and beat the dog every day, obviously with no reason. You might say, well no one does that without reason. I tell you everyone, including me, has done that sometime or the other with the poor creatures. Well, they do not get this trait if you beat them once or twice. Like, you will not become Usain Bolt if you run the hundred meters only once or twice in your life. So, you will have to beat them every day. Now, what do you expect the dog to grow up like? Well, studies show that hurting a dog can increase its aggression, lower the quality of interaction with other dogs and human beings. Similarly, showing extensive love and care to them makes them more affectionate, loyal and dedicated partners. A dog treated like a pet, will remain a pet. A dog treated like a friend will become a friend.

Anyhow, it's not some people's fault that they didn't know that beating and behaving badly with the dogs makes them aggressive and harmful. Now, to decrease this aggression and make the dogs harmless the intelligent vets have come up with an easy-peasy solution. They say, if they will spay the females and neuter the males, or in other words, castrate the poor creatures, their aggressiveness can be controlled to an extent that you will fall in love with the politeness of them dogs.

Well, how inhumane it may sound, this is what our qualified, well-educated, animal-loving, passionate and dedicated vets have to say. How about we neuter the masters in first-place and the problem will not arise at all. The shenanigans behind neutering the pets has spread all over the community and has been taken up as a very suitable solution to the problem. A problem that is created by us, the humans. Anyhow, no dog can read my book and that you too are a human, I can't risk offending you. And in any case, I don't want to curse our own species that I have a load of respect for.

But to have respect for the whole species and to have it for a bunch of idiots is a whole different thing. I respect the species as a whole. That doesn't mean I respect what any selfish, self-centered fucker wants to do. Especially, if that fucker inhibits the natural behavior of an organism by removing the functioning organs that is a requisite not only for aggression or reproduction, but also for intelligence and dedication toward living. In a first, what I feel is that the brains of these idiot vets need to be removed. I mean they aren't able to use it properly and have become aggressive toward the dogs. They can't even come up with a constructive solution to the problem at hand using that ganglion of theirs. They are a lazy bunch of ass-holes who have found the easiest solution; just remove the balls. Well, leave the vets. I want to talk about the masters. They let the vets talk them into this crime against the nature. I know they are naïve and do not know a thing about what they are doing. Well, this is a good excuse for any crime ever committed. But shouldn't there be a way of taking a consent from some authority? Sadly, there is no such law that stops this nuisance. Oh! Wait. I think there is one. The AVMA, American Veterinary Medical Association, makes it mandatory in some states to spay/neuter the pets before the age of four months. Can you imagine? The extent of shenanigans we have entered into.

Only those who love dogs should be bothered. No? It is not about dog lovers or dog haters. It is about the level we humans have stooped down to control other species out of fear. Well, I will leave this topic here. I don't want to conclude anything out of it. I just was clarifying what in the hell was wrong with my neighbor's dog. The poor dog was neutered, recently. Most probably the surgery was successful, but since the dog was an adult its reaction to it was rage and anger, but now sadly not like in its previous ballsy days.

Chapter 4

FIGHT or FLIGHT

I remember my body was in a strange mode. Of all the modes I can only relate mine with the mighty, the mode of all the modes, the fight or flight mode. Since most of us are already familiar with this mode, let me just brush up the basics on that. If there is anything you can do about this mode when it gets switched on, it is just that you can sit back, if possible, relax and experience the ride. I have found that this mode is very underrated in the science community. I guess, any topic in its parent field is almost always underrated. Like, take Alexander the Great for an instance. After all his accomplishments and achievements, his mom still must have been like, "Oh! Alex? He used to be a very timid boy. I don't know why, but I guess he still is shy in front of them girls." For the happiness of the heavens, I am just glad, she is no more. I mean, I think she was mortal. With she gone, no one can mess with the legend. So, anyone from the science community, and biology to be precise, is already opinionated about this fight or flight mode or any other fucking mode for that matter.

I hear these experts on the TV saying stuff like this, "We do not even use a full ten percent of our brain's capacity." Well, it is not true. The brain is involved in so many functions and at frequencies, the instruments of these so-called experts are not calibrated to receive a signal from. They are overly confident of what they have found out in a period of a few decades. And that is somehow not dangerous but is really stupid to sit on. This over-confidence is what inhibits and abases the growth of our knowledge of such subjects.

So, don't be fooled by what those cocky experts have to say. Do not ask an expert about anything ever. You are bound to lose the charm of the first-hand experience. It is like asking an astronaut the feel of the empty space. You see, his suit is too lousy to give him the real taste of that free and empty pocket of infinity. The astronaut must hate his lousy suit, for that matter. So close, yet so far. They don't say it, but I tell you they are fucking frustrated. It is in their eyes. And the experts, they are so worse than them zebras, I tell you. To exaggerate the situation, you can never forget the moment your body enters this mode. That moment is like magic. I mean words are so weak.

I don't know the key to hold your thoughts and make you look at yourself, before I can merely try and break that immensely mind fucking and killer feeling that it makes you experience. Anyways, I can't hold you from anything ever. So, it feels like the pilot, that's you, being forced out of the cockpit. And cockpit?

Yeah, that's your fucking body. When this auto-mode kicks in, you are somewhere out. The thing is we think that it is not possible to get out of the Universe. Oh! Well, we just think. Though, the pilot resists, cries, and even tries to sabotage the operation as a whole, but that, that my friend will be of little to no use. The body, that you thought was you all along this so-called life, starts defying all the known rules. The notion that we know more than our body, is shattered in that one moment. Some accept it, some resist. And that creates the fucking problem. You know how they have treated the guys who stood up for resistance. The body knows better. Better than you, me or that professor of physiology. It takes over, whenever and wherever it feels this mode is now needed. The fact is, it has been wrongly termed as fight or flight mode. It should be what-the-fuck-can-you-do-now mode. Practically, you cannot do anything about it. You may feel that it's 'you' reading this book right now, and not your eyes, from where the neurons take that info with lightning speed to the processors of the brain, that convert the image into something understandable, which then is synthesized by the cerebral explosions, signaling the hippocampus to pick up the exact emotion for precisely that fucking line, that your eyes zeroed in and focused on, from where your motion receptors take a signal to another department from where the facial muscles are controlled, that finally brings a smile on your face. You may be deluded by the fact that this all being is done by you. The great you. It will take a whole library of the NYU neurological department to precisely tell you, just how you read a word and reacted to it. This is true for everything we do, everything we think, and how we react to things. According to the experts, the fight or flight mode comes handy when we are in some sort of danger. Well, life is all fucking dangerous. As Jim Rohn puts it, "Let me tell you how risky life is. You are not getting out alive."

By this, I came to a very old thought that I discussed with one of my friends, and who ironically, of all the sane things I had told him, remembers this one clearly to this very day. I was conversing with him on phone, and as usual I was trying to chisel something out of what we were talking about. I like doing that. Like, I cannot have a shallow conversation in person or on phone. It doesn't sadden me to do that, I do talk just about anything unimportant sometimes, but mostly I try to find some point in that too. So, in some small development during the conversation, I told him that when we are alone, we become two. I mean, when we are sitting alone in our rooms and not listening to anything, not reading anything, not watching television, but just sitting and contemplating about something, who are we in dialogue with? That is to say we create two people out of one. Now, it is impossible to do that with another person. You will never be able to talk to the other self of someone else. Unless, the other person is Jim Carrey. You can talk to a thousand people by just talking to this person. So, when you are alone you are in a dialogue with yourself. It sounds mad, as it is a socially accepted as a taboo to talk to yourself for long periods of time. But that is not an issue here. Taboos are created to enjoy them more exclusively. Like if sex is enjoyed exactly like food on the dinner table, with the whole family, or is made as casual as an evening walk, the population will make a sharp dip. It is only because of its tabooed status, that people find a thrill in participating in sexual behaviors more and more around the globe. Resistance is the key to the success of every taboo.

All the Freudians know there can only be a philosophical explanation to such inquiries. No experiment, practical or supernatural, statistical or gooey, can bring a conclusion to such remarks. Well, it's not new to mankind encounter a few participating in long hours of contemplations with the self. Recently, the psychologists have shown that most successful people go into recesses created only for some time in solitude.

Even when we are not to make it deliberate, every person, when alone, talks to the self by default. There is no question about this. It is only that people do not know it first thing, and secondly if they come to know they find it awkward to discuss it with others. But it is as natural as taking a leak in the secluded cubical in the washrooms. What do we do when we are peeing alone, do we stop the conversation completely we were having with someone before that or do we talk to ourselves? And while doing that we sometimes come to a better solution or take on the topic of the discussions. Not only in solitude, we do it even while in conversation with others. We have politely named this activity as, lost in them thoughts. But if we are sincere enough to address that as a careful dialogue with the self, it turns out to be a sort of meditation. It's all in naming what you do. Sigmund Freud named three selves, Id, Ego and Superego. Well, according to him the Id and the Superego are the extremes and the Ego had the liberty to oscillate from one to another, while enjoying all the bandwidth between the two.

So, when we are completely alone, and I mean completely, no television, no social media, no mobile phones, no books and no self-pleasing activities, only the complete you with the complete natural environment, an environment that is free from any man-made shit, when we enter such an environment, there starts a dialogue deep inside of us. This dialogue isn't like the one you had while peeing, or while you were sitting alone in that party. This dialogue is the purest of all. The gurus call it meditation. You will not have to stop yourself from thinking any particular thought. You just have to enter in such an environment.

Though, in today's life this kind of environment is highly improbable to get on a daily basis, but with some efforts one can reach there. One can go out for a walk, sit silently somewhere, go for a drive, or even lay down on the bed with eyes fixed on the ceiling. Just anything whatever is possible can be done to reach yourself.

And when we reach there, a dialogue begins between the Id and the Superego. This dialogue is only listened by the Ego. Also, while it listens, it does not participate in the dialogue. It means it listens to the dialogue, takes lesson from it and then apply it in the dialogues with others. We can say the Ego is the representative of both the Id and the Superego.

Coming back to the fight or flight mode. It is somewhere deep seeded in a person's that inner dialogue, that when this mode kicks in does he stay put and fight, or rather just fly from the scene. If the Ego has long listened to the dialogue with patience and is now comfortable in coming out in the open with others, there will be a great amount of resistance put by it. This resistance, like all the others, will be painful by nature in the beginning. Slowly it will become the second nature and after some time it will be long forgotten. Imagine a tree that manages to reach a height way above the ground. It will have to bear the weight of its branches, leaves, fruits and all the fauna that will use it as their home. The tree endures through the pain simultaneously making its roots reach deeper, trunk thicker, and balance of right amount and measure. It does this so that it can reach that perfect height, support all the possible weight and then come to fruition. Once it is able to support a certain amount of weight at a certain amount of height, it doesn't have to do it again and again, but will just retain it like its second nature. The tree only grows from there. It forgets the weight it has added to itself in years but is still able to carry it. Similarly, the fight we put in one area of life may not be fruitful in the beginning, but when enduring through it we are able to reach a comfortable height and support the weight, we can enjoy the fruits of our own trees.

But if there is a shortage of the dialogues between the Id and the Superego, the Ego will act as a shunt. It will let the current bypass without deriving any sort of useful work out of it. When the Ego chooses the first option, fighting, instead of taking a flight, the decisions at first seem a bit annoying and even impossible. But it is all about the dialogue. The Ego will choose the fight option only when it has patiently listened to the dialogue in solitude. Then it knows the outcome before even the first step toward that climb is even taken.

Chapter 5

The TREE of PAIN

S o, I was about to get up from my then lying-on-the-bed position, when it dawned upon me that it wasn't just another headache. I mean, like the ones we all get. The ones that we wish would go away with a pill or two. The ones which have helped the pharmaceutical industry swell like a giant blubber. The ones we have when we miss our morning tea or when we miss the absence of that smart-ass in the office. The ones we have, when we sleep a few extra hours on those slothful Sundays. The ones that come so slow that we can't see them coming, and go so fast, that we can't say a goodbye to. But this, this was the one that I knew at once that it didn't come to stay or go anywhere. It was like it came in a bang, and I knew it was everywhere in the same instant. Something like that happens only once in a lifetime. Like you go before you come. Or something eaten even before it was cooked. Or die before you live. There was in reality no pain. What I was experiencing was the aftermath of this micro-bang.

The time of birth is very painful, both, for the child as well as the mother. But since the baby's pain receptors in her brain are still to develop in order to respond to that pain, all the newborns go through this phase of getting born virtually without any memory of it. Mother, on the other hand, will have an imprint of their first experience of giving birth and her brain will adjust to the pain once she goes through it. Since the mother has gone through the process once already, the second time is relatively easier and most of the second births are less painful as well as less fatal. Although, the pain incurred is the same, but since the mother put a fight in her first delivery, her pain receptors that are now resilient to the incoming pain signals, modify them into something else and thus the delivery feels a lot less painful this time.

This is all very natural, and millions of years spent in the evolution have made pain a necessary part of any sort of growth. Pain, as popularly described as something evil, is the first sign of birth and growth. Although, in some cases it relates to death and disease too, but that accounts for the pain that was not incurred in one's life deliberately. The deliberation of inflicting pain on ourselves is the cure to any outside pain that we may encounter mentally, physically or emotionally.

We humans, unlike the other animals, have the power of choice. And since it is not known how much we need to undergo to achieve something, we all know roughly the price of a good life inertly. What a good life is, is a question that is different to everybody, but something is common in every answer. For me, a good life is the one in which we can do things our way. Now there are various ways of interpreting that, but a very accurate explanation can be that if you want to do something, and if in the course of doing that thing you know there will be some pain that you will have to encounter, and if you are free to experience that pain on your own will and choice, the fruits you will bear after this will all be sweeter individually than all the pain you endured combined.

Now, there are a number of pains that you may encounter. The pain of rejection, the pain of separation, physical pain, mental pain, psychoanalytical pain, and many other forms. All these kinds of pains are to make our whole system strong and firm. Going through it all, one comes out as a totally different human being.

When the deliberation to inflict pain on ourselves is weak, or to put it like we only choose what is easier and painless, the outcome is always very less appealing to us. It is when we choose those small tough things every day, that are difficult to deal with, and choose to break our heads against a wall that seems impossible to be broken, then the formation of pain begins. This formation of pain gets stored in form of growth in our minds. We might seem to achieve nothing practically, but somewhere deep the will to reach there will grow out of you. Just like the roots and the trunk of the tree, your mind is getting stronger and stronger. Since we are humans and are always just an arm's distance away from the gift of choice, there are always multiple reasons to give up and just continue with an average life. Not because we want this kind of life or that we love it, but because our mind tricks us to make a choice that is very easy to grasp, but since it is a short cut, that many before us have taken, that is what leads us to a public park. Public park is metaphorically used to describe the bottom of the pyramid.

In his poem, "the road not taken," by Robert Frost, he starts from talking about taking a path that has not been taken by many before and ends it by talking about all the difference it has made. The formative curve of everyone's life is defined by the choices they make in the times of difficulties. The choice to keep running when we are on a brink of collapsing, when the remaining distance is as long as what we have completed yet. The choice of going for the interview that we are sure that we are going to get rejected. The choice of taking a step in a direction when you have no knowledge of reaching the final destination. The choice of speaking up for yourself in front of people you admire knowing that might hurt them. The choice of going up to that someone you love and declare to them your love for them, even when your heart is pounding out of the fear of rejection, ignorance or even mockery.

All these acts are not only because of bravery, but in times of adversity and hopelessness, the actor has to become prescient too. Studies have found that being brave and simultaneously being prescient, that is to see a positive outcome beforehand, is an important key to success. Now by being prescient, I do not say that you have to become a shaman or a pawing. What it means is that for that moment, out of all the thoughts that run through our minds, if we hold on that beautiful outcome and truly believe in it, we will only see wonders happening. Now, that is really not that simple. You might say, what if I get rejected after that interview? Or what if I get rejected by someone who was at least hanging out with me as a friend? Well, that is true, you will get hurt if the outcome is negative. But again, if we go back to the reference of the tree, and ask ourselves this, that what if the tree says, "NO! NO MORE BRANCHES! I HAVE HAD ENOUGH AND I AM CONTENT WITH WHATEVER AMOUNT OF SUNLIGHT I AM GETTING!" Well that will be a big shame. Because if the tree doesn't grow a branch and doesn't risk growing in the direction of more light, it will risk a bigger thing; its existence. Maybe we are risking our existence by not risking our ego to be exposed to a small amount of pain. A little adventure here and there every day isn't a joke, it is a necessity. As Jim Rohn says, "It's better to live thirty years full of adventure, than to live a hundred safe in the corner." Risking and making difficult choices, however hard, however painful, will always lead us to beautiful destinations that only some brave and prescient beings can reach.

The thing that a very few people realize is that these painful decisions can only be accrued in small quantities on a daily basis. If the growth has to be fast and if it happens overnight, the glory doesn't last for long. No one can fall into success suddenly. Similarly, no one falls into failure suddenly. It is a summation of all the small and big decisions that we have made throughout our lives that lead us to where we are today or will be tomorrow. These decisions, though however easy or difficult to make, are the crucial building blocks of our persona. Knowledge of the dangerous information of falling at hand, and still willing to take a leap of faith is what adventure is all about.

When I was bitten by a snake, it was an experience out of this world. From the moment I knew that there was a snake in that room to the time when I was bitten, as I grabbed its tail, my mind was blocked by any negative thought about the event. I was young, twenty-three, and since my childhood I had a wish to encounter a snake. I am always cautious of what I wish for, because as Rumi says, "What you are seeking is also seeking you." It is true. Anyway, that experience was one in a billion that I still remember to this day. Not because I was bitten by the cobra, but because I managed to grab its tail for a femtosecond. The crowd which was gathered to see the snake was now seeing an event where a young man dared to catch hold the tail of a cobra and was bitten by it. I was laughed upon too. The shopkeeper, where the incident happened, threw me out of his shop out of the fear that I might have died in there. My dear friends who were amongst the onlookers rushed me to a nearby hospital. From there I was shifted to the second hospital as the first one did not have the anti-snake venom to treat me. Over there I was a star patient. Every kind of doctor was visiting my bed to check on the first case of snakebite in their hospital. I was a case study for a dozen of new and old doctors. However weak and clumsy, I could feel the amount of adrenaline that was rushing up and down my blood stream.

After a week or two, when I was home, I was getting visitors at my home from my relatives to my friends, to my parents' friends and their colleagues. It was a sort of celebrity mode that I just entered because of that single, though crazy but tough decision of grabbing the cobra's tail. I don't mean to say that it was a very wise thing to do. I could have died in the process or could have harmed myself in some other way. But again, it was a necessary part of my being.

Taking decisions that seem crazy in the beginning, but if deep inside you have a feeling that this is one of those things that need to be done to reach that final place, we should encourage ourselves to take those decisions on a routine basis.

Chapter 6

The MISSING COMB

Though my headache must have stayed for just a billionth of a femtosecond, it almost felt like an eternity. It seemed as if the time has stopped and I had entered in some non-time dimension. I am a very lousy thinker. You can catch me thinking about almost anything. The major block that stops us from thinking most of the times is that when we grow older, we start fearing the uselessness of spending our precious time on thinking. Thinking, is a very powerful tool, as we all know. But it is not limited to those like, Aristotle, Galileo, or Socrates. It is a tool available to all of us, inherently. Think of it as exercise is to body, thinking is to brain. Now, when you train your body by running in circles, you surely don't assume that you are doing something useless. Well, if seen from one aspect, lifting weights, running on a treadmill, dancing on a song are inherently useless activities. But they surely help us revive us to a state where our body starts responding productively to situations that demand some form of physical work. Similarly, thinking is training your brain for situations where you will be able to navigate through situations that require some thought more efficiently and faster. In order to fool the grown-up brain, we need to tell it some lies. Lies that are not harmful but are there to help in the construction of a better and healthier brain. Ever saw those supporting frames, that support a freshly constructed building? Those are not going to stay with the building forever. Once the building starts to support its weight, they get removed.

There is this word 'pseudologia fantastica', in the psychological community. It is used for people who lie to other people for the fun of it. It isn't that they want to hurt other people, but they can't help but lie, just for the kick of it. So, considering it some sort of madness, psychologists have classified it as a legit mental illness. That is completely fine, because some people get caught up in the act of lying forever. But if taken in small quantity and used in a way that it serves some purpose like a medicine, pseudologia fantastica is very useful. Whenever we encounter a difficult situation, a voice echoes from somewhere which says that we can't overcome this situation. Now, it is nothing but the Id talking to the Ego. But if we can only for that time fool ourselves by lying to ourselves and listen to the Superego instead, we will feel energetic and motivated to go through the same situation.

As I was saying, I am a very generous thinker. Generous guys are lousy, all the time. So, once I was thinking about the comb. Yes, about the comb that is right now lying with another comb in billions of drawers around the globe. The same comb that you comb your hair with. I cannot say why I was thinking about it. All I know is that it was not my fault. Maybe it was lying on my table in my office, and I just combed away my awesome hair and may have wondered about this canine tool. Anyway, I may have a solid reason for that thought. I had this job. I used to teach the already enlightened undergraduate students of engineering. Can you imagine? Nobody can teach them. Nobody, I tell you. Teaching human beings, then teaching those who think that they can become engineers by doing engineering. You see? In India we do engineering. We do not study or pursue engineering studies. We do it. Like, we do shit, we do the do. If anywhere you will find an amazing usage of this language, like this, in this Universe, it is here in India. And if you want to see miracles that can liberate your stupid insecure mind, come to the department of Mechanical Engineering. Come to this department, may it be in any university or college in India. We all follow English medium. And yes, we do engineering. I am already done. I mean I have already done the doing part. So, teaching those enlightened sons of guns was like putting my tool for a slight taper on the lathe. And when I used to get fucking bored of tapering it, in my breaks, I used to sit on my work station and research the goddam Google. You see anything you search on google is already searched by some smart-ass out there. So, in almost ninety nine percent cases you are researching. If anything, that can take over the planet by its collar, it is this goddam Google. Sometimes I imagine God googling up Himself. Though, He won't be disappointed totally.

Anyway, so I was thinking about the comb in that break. And then, I googled up the bloody comb. I read its history, like when we started combing our hair, and what were the early combs made up of. Like, the rich must have had combs made up of gold, diamond and what not, while the poor must have used the wooden ones, or the ones made up of stone. Ah! Stone combs! That really sounds heavy to the head. And I wondered, whether a comb could be a manifestation of God himself. Like, Jesus had long hair and all. Two things never lie. Shakira's hips and the church. And I have seen Jesus there. I mean in the church. Like in the pictures. He has been portrayed way to serious though. As if something had been bothering the young man all along. But one of my dope friends told me, that Jesus looks at you in the same mood that you are in. And the moment he told me I fucking googled up Jesus. Seriously, he isn't at all serious. He isn't sad. He isn't happy. Well, I was stoned at that time. And, forgive me, Jesus did look stoned. But he the point is that he had long hair. Did he comb his hair with a comb? Or did he go for a brush, or his fingers. I am pretty sure he must have been a very charming man. And using your hands to do your hair, time and again, in a conversation is very common. My wife uses a brush, most of the times.

Anyway, that used to really piss my employers off. Like, you can deal with porn, Facebook, and other internet breaches that can really help build a case against an employee to let him go. But how do you fire a guy, who googles up the goddam comb and its history, for fuck sake? I didn't use the f word. I believe my employers did. So, while combing through the results I figured out that comb's history, like any other, is sort of unclear. It seemed to be all under cover kind of. I don't blame Wikipedia for that. Like my dear Wiki has a history for everything. I mean the history column on every page, but for comb, the story is little. May be like so many other things, the church didn't want us to know the truth behind the comb either. So, it just said this, "Combs have been used by humans since prehistoric times, having been discovered in very refined forms from settlements dating back to 5000 years ago in Persia." Really? Is that all you got for the poor comb? But I am almost always immune to getting pissed off. Like, the only thing next to the zebra, that can piss me off, is me. So, I started imagining the Persian king, Xerxes, combing his hair. Needless to say, the imagination was ported to the time before he dipped himself in that pool filled with some kind of super hair removal solution. I mean he enjoyed a hell in his life, before Leonidas fucked up his mind and all, if that remained at all after that dipping scene, but his hair? I really feel pity for him. Well, if I would have been Xerxes though, I would have done almost anything to save my facial and pubic hair at least. Who can deny the fullness and sponged up feel that one gets from the beard and the pubic. The guys in the porn? They are just a show and are fucked up when it comes to hair. Like, fucked up apart from their career goals. Just know that it is appealing only to others when you shave off the goddam pubic. If anything is important on this body after the rolled-up fist with a hole, it is the pubic. Why do you think Xerxes was busy organizing the goddam orgies even as the war was on?

Anyway, it was his truth. But far from blaming the Wiki, I feel I was like in debt for its generosity. It at least, gives a fuck to the poor comb. I do. I would have felt so lonely, if I was to find nothing about the goddam comb, on the fucking Internet. Technically, Internet is some thirty odd years old. So am I. And I first started off with this rascal, in 2006 A.D. I know it was fucking late. When I was still busy collecting magazines, newspapers and at last relying only on my own imagination, my friends and college-mates had already juiced out a hundred and fifty liters from their balls using this miraculous rascal. That time is again a thing that I miss now. As I started off, that day with the Internet, I believe, since then there had been hardly any day, that I did not surf it or my own manhood with it. I miss the imagination part. You see, it is something that you cannot control. You cannot control the missing part. You cannot control what you can miss. And me? I can miss almost anything. You name it, and I can miss it. Missing is a feeling that is indeed a very modern one, I am sure. At times, I am sure of things, that I am sure of. So, unlike pain, happiness, and grief, missing is really modern. It is like a flirtation with all the feelings combined. Humans, the modern ones, can miss almost anything. Like, I can miss the time when I was happy, when I was sad, or when I was fucking angry on myself. What I have found is that missing is an irrelevant, time killing emotion. Erma Bombeck quoted, "Worry is like a rocking chair. It gives you something to do, but never gets you anywhere." But missing something, or someone is worse. Like the seasons; you will miss winters in summers, and summers in winters. No one knows why that happens, but it does. You will always find someone whining about the weather and wishing for the one that they were whining about when it was there. Well, it is a very unrealistic emotion. You cannot miss the future. But you can be happy, be sad, fear, or even enjoy that is still to come. See, missing something is completely absurd. But we love to miss. I love missing a lot. It is like one of my favorite time munchies. I think you are getting, where I am strolling you to.

Chapter 7

CRYING for the VISA

Coming back to the main reason. The reason why I started writing this book. So, as I was getting up from the bed. I felt like my eyes were wet and all. I don't know if you have ever experienced anything like this ever. Like you are crying, and you do not know that you are, but somehow your body knows that you are crying. It is giving you the symptoms that you are in the very process of missing something, but this time it is really going to get you somewhere. Where it will lead you will all depend on how you will plan the course ahead. The body, being a connected organism, knows you have lost something very precious back in the sand of time. And the next thing you come to know that all this time when you were being happy and all very playful, you were living one big lie. You find that the flirting with missing and all suddenly got real. You will not want to mess with missing and all any time after this. Like, it is so easy to understand, and so true that at some level or the other we all are living a lie. I'll use a contrived example given by Neil deGrasse Tyson here. Imagine a spelling bee contest. There are three kids who are asked to spell the word, 'cat.' The first spells it, as c-a-t, the second spells it, as k-a-t, and the third spells it, x-q-h. Now, as we can see the first one hit the bull's eye. Both the second and third are wrong, but to what degree? How wrong is the second one from the third one? If we look up the dictionary, the second one is more correct than the first one, because the dictionary uses the same spelling to define the word phonetically. But since we have to follow an organized accord to fit in the society, to survive, both the second as well as the third kid are given the same treatment. Some make peace with it, and some will fight with it. It is best to keep fighting though, until what-the-fuck-can-you-do-now mode doesn't kick in. Everybody will face that sooner or later. Anything that happens to you while you are alive is never late. Something cool happened in those moments with me. I came to know of my condition slightly later than my body knew it. Like, a billionth of a femtosecond later. You may say, that was nothing and I could have easily caught up back with it. But no, by then my body had already started adjusting to the new shift. Adjusting on its own self. I always believed you do not need to travel centuries back to travel in time. All you need a slight shift in time. What you need is that the time you perceive and the time that you live in somehow, both get back into orientation. Like you are living on a different time scale and your body on a different one. Strolling here and there your whole life, you come on the same page once and for all. Anyway, I do not want to make it a heavy dose for you. Anyhow, life goes on and there will be more of such femtoseconds to realize.

So, as the moment took on, I was filling the space ahead with my being. I was literally travelling in time. I pulled my hands to the front. All I wanted to feel was my own eyes, that couldn't see anything clearly. Moments ago, I was lying on my bed, suddenly my eyes were flushing out tears apparently for no solid reason. You see, if anything in life stands strong apart from death, it is the reason itself. No body no mind and no soul will be able to find the reason for its own self. The body finds the reason for the mind, and the mind finds the reason for the soul and the soul frees itself the moment it knows it. It takes a flight so high and so long, and so deep and so short, that a femtosecond will seem to be like an eternity, and the eternity will fit into that femtosecond itself. But the reason is imperative. You can kill a wave, skip a beat, mechanize a rhythm and even stop the ticking time itself, but honestly you will need a reason to do so.

As I was trying to touch my eyes with my fingers, I started to burst into this unrealistic mode of crying. By now I thought it was just that I was crying for something. Something that I didn't have any clue of. And as I was nearing the emotion that was so obvious, a tear just oozed out of my right eye. It cleared the vision and I could see my fingers coming into my eyes. In the same moment, which must have been again shorter than a billionth of a femtosecond,

I was somehow able to analyze that this unrealistic mode of crying was not crying but weeping. I will try and tell how these two differ. (I know you know them both differently. So please feel free to skip to the next line. I don't know which one.) So, coming to the difference. Crying is the most common of all emotions. We cry all the time, like when we are hurt, or when someone leaves us in the rut for life. We cry when we feel betrayed or when life doesn't give us what we want. That sums up a very little part of all the crying that goes around in this world all day and all night long. Right now, a child is crying for a toy, a lady is crying about a relationship, a man is crying for mercy somewhere in this world. Crying is sometimes also attributed to apparently no fucking reason. In a party a bunch of joyful people can be addressed by some irritated soul, "These ass-holes are all over the place, crying like fucking idiots." But weeping? Weeping, my friend, is not at all like crying. It is the scariest of all the things on this planet. It is the darkest of all the sadness this Universe has to offer. Weeping, I tell you, is scarier than the fucking death itself. If death is the choice of the millions who commit suicide at any given time, why do you think it becomes their choice at last? It is fucking easier to die and get rid of this weeping, than to face it for the rest of your life. Grief, my friend is darker than darkness itself. Only some very determined and wilful joy can light up the room, in which grief makes a temporary stay. But there's no sound louder than the silence of grief. Weeping, my friend, is no sister of crying. It is the mother of all the grief. It is the truth that blossoms only when you aren't ready for it. Yes, that's the point. It doesn't want you to be ready for it. No matter what you do, no matter how ready you try to be, it will catch you in that billionth of a femtosecond. In that moment where you will be most absent of its existence. Like, if you want it, you will get it, but more importantly it will come to you if you deserve it. I have had a long debate with myself on this wanting and deserving thing that goes on in this game of life and death. Life gives you what you deserve, and but no one knows what they deserve. Knowing what you want is easy, but knowing what you deserve, requires a great amount of time spent with your own very self. You will not agree, if I say that you deserve the whole Universe in that billionth of a femtosecond. I mean all the world in that single instant. All you will say is that you deserve peace and happiness. Every great scripture professes that we are the Universe itself, but it is not easy to hold that thought for long or forever. It is difficult but not impossible.

So, I realized I was fucking weeping. It was all weird. You can imagine how weird it was getting. A guy smokes up weed and goes to bed. He wakes up, freshens up. Then, he pushes for a happy meal and jerks off to the fountain of happiness. All is so goddam smooth. Nothing in reality to get bothered about. The guy is happy. Very determined to live. Live a life most of the people can only imagine of. The closest one can get is shagging off to the strength of the last drop left in those two balls dangling below the tool. How about it is already, juiced out? Will you dare go for it then? No. Most will wait for a refill. Me? Not at all. It was like the most urgent of all the tasks. Balls had to take care of the juice themselves. I didn't care if there was any at all. As Shakira cried, "Whenever! Wherever!" And next I realized that I am lying on the bed, trying to get up from my bed, weeping and all. Weeping? Good Lord! I was weeping for the heaven's sake! Let's save the fuck sake for the fuck sake this time. I don't know if anyone other than me will be able to make peace with the kind of arrangement in which it happened to me. I mean, I know that we are all born in a very customized setting, and of course those settings are unique to all. And everyone has their own way to free their souls and all, but mine was still weird. Like Buddha was walking in the lush green jungles of Himalayas, when he got his peace. Swami Vivekananda was sitting in the feet of his Guru, when his soul was freed, while Jesus was born with the silver spoon, but me? Well, I do not think little of my arrangement or otherwise. What is weird today might not be weird tomorrow, but it still remains weird for today. Though I cannot think of any other moment which would have been perfect for it to happen. Basically, it is about happening. Who cares, how and when? How and when is for those who are still in the queue. Imagine yourself in a long queue at a busy visa office. All you need to know in that queue from someone, who is just like you, that how will it happen, how much time it will take, and whether you will get that stamp or not on your passport. Irony is that the guy you ask, also wants to know the answers to the same questions. The only thing that really matters is that you do not want to mess with the fucking visa officer, for the fuck sake. In that queue you can only do one thing. Wait. Rest all is the manifestation of your wiggly mind. It pops up one thought after another. And the poor brain fires up the neurons that have no business in the process of your visa approval. Deep down you know the only thing that you do not want to do is to mess with the visa officer. So, you will ask for anything at all that you feel is relevant to the process, but finally that won't matter at all when your visa will be approved. Maybe that's the only reason you have picked up this book in the first place. But I can assure you even if you haven't picked it and haven't read it till here, it won't matter, after once your visa is approved.

Chapter 8

MOSQUITO BITES

So, after I realized I was in this grief mode, my fingers finally reached my eyes. I started rubbing them with my all so caressing fingers.

As I told earlier, the time factor for me, then, was not at all that I had experienced ever before that goddam headache. Like, experiencing pain in reverse so that you can experience joy in forward, simultaneously. Like, when we commit a crime, and we know deep in our hearts that one day it will all be coming back to us. Just because, our self-pity is so strong that we are able to make them look like just a few silly innocent mistakes of our ignorant being. As if, they came along in this fucking package, called life. The mistake to see the nature as something other than us. Or to be precise, seeing it is as our enemy. I used to see mosquitoes as the little devils from the hell itself. It was such a fun to clap one of these to death anytime I could. I couldn't resist the temptation to kill them, even when the poor guys were off-duty; sitting somewhere and smoking a joint on a wall. And if I ever did spot them, it used to be the last joint of their life. And the joy of splashing one red blot of my own blood, on my one hand with my another, as the devil was still in the process of biting me, knew no boundaries. It seemed to be my duty to save myself from almost anything that nature had to offer. And because I was the devil myself, I saw the mosquitoes too as devils who took pleasure in biting us. By the way, a mosquito has a fucking straw that dangles out from its mouth like a cigar. With that, it has been biting us from eons. I really admire the quote, "Half knowledge is dangerous." I believe it is more than just dangerous. It has been fatal for the poor mosquitoes. They have been using the straw to bite us just like I have been using my car to fly to the moon and back. Leaving the drama, they suck the fucking blood out of us with that straw. They suck it with far more care than that fat-assed nurse who sticks a needle in the ass. The needle that is hundred times thicker than the mosquito's straw. And the bitch gets paid to do that stuff. Well, it's all politics. We have been made to believe that the mosquitoes bite us and not suck on us, by a few smart-ass humans. You know why? Because that somehow aggravates the already itchy reputation, these poor creatures have been awarded. It helps inflate the mosquito's status to a bigger bad-ass devil. It helps make them a nightmare, make them look like the high-class vampires, that bite into our flesh. Whereas the poor fellows, have only a fucking straw that dangles down from their mouth. My wife is a dentist and she has validated the fact. She told me, "She never had a patient that was a mosquito, one. The straw like thing that dangles out, is known as proboscis, two. So technically it cannot bite." I was not surprised when she told me this. As before asking this, I googled up the fact on my own. I told you, I am the devil. And, all this time the poor mosquito has been just putting its fucking proboscis into our already good-for-nothing skin, to reach the eternal pool of blood. It doesn't even start hurting before it drinks the required amount, that is not more than five micro liters of blood. Fuck! Can you believe that? Five fucking micro liters! And I used to clap them all to death just for this volume. I guess they should put up two solid cases against us, the humans, in the courtroom of nature. One for that they have been wrongly awarded the status of canines. And two, the volume of blood that they suck up in one serving is too less, rather negligible, for someone to lose any amount of blood that can lead to death. And killing them for it, is inmosquito, if not inhuman. By the way, I believe, in a way, they already have filed these two cases. We'll know in time, that they are winning too. Nature has a habit of making collaborative existence. In biology it is known as mutualism. The most common example for mutualism the zoologists give is that of the rhino and the oxpecker. Oxpecker, a bird, is often seen on those wild television shows, riding on the back of a rhino that lazes in a marsh. They both have something to gain out of each other. The oxpecker eats away all the parasites that otherwise are impossible for the rhino to remove individually by itself. The oxpecker gets a meal and the rhino gets relief from the parasites. In the wild, these kinds of mutualisms are very common and are found almost with every animal alive, big or small.

Now, you must be thinking that the mosquito is also a parasite and since we do not have a friend like the mighty oxpecker, this is a matter that needs to be taken in our own hands. Thus, killing the goddam mosquitoes is a service to the humanity after all. Well, that is not entirely true. Yes, the mosquitoes are parasites, as obviously they are the blood-suckers. But we too have a few oxpeckers that come and live with us to safeguard us from them mosquitoes. Like the spider, or the lizard. They both do not do any harm to us directly. They live in safe distant corners of the house, perfectly safe from us. But what do we do? We remove them too using every possible means made available to us. All we do is act as we are told. Told by our parents and told by our society. A society that is ruled by a bunch of idiots nowadays. I really do not see a reason why the mutualism, that our ancestors survived with in all those millions of years, has suddenly become a nightmare for us humans?

The posit I am trying to make here is that we humans are slowly forgetting the very basics of life and the means to survive in the natural environment. It is true that we too, are nature. But like the above example, we are trying to bring down the parasites, the friends and somehow the whole fauna, on our own. By taking matters entirely in our own hands we are inhibiting the process of mutualism. This inhibition isn't just something that will stay only to the mosquitoes or the spider or the lizard. It is slowly seeping deep in our own psyche.

Mosquitoes aren't going to vanish. I am not concerned about them mosquitoes. They are doing well, and they will continue to do well. After all we aren't the only hot-blooded mammals out here. There are a million different species they can choose from. Slowly but surely, we humans have started to disconnect from the nature. It is a paradox to say that though. I have always seen a human being a part of the nature. But somehow, the power and the freedom of choice that it has been gifted with has started to become its weakness and we are creating our own tiny prison.

Lately, in a race to earn a living we have transformed everything that is natural around us into something artificial and unhealthy. We are running around in haste to find the perfect solution to the miseries we have created by refusing the generous help that nature wants to offer. Instead of taking its helping hand by bending down to our knees, we humans have decided to go on in our own artificial ways. The rivers have turned into canals. The mountains into pyramids. The lakes into swimming pools. And the mosquitoes into politicians. Well, that's just a way I feel. I have no grudge against them politicians. They are always very polite and that is what counts for in today's life. A big round-faced polite ass-hole makes a hell of a politician.

The resources, as per the statistics, are limited for us today. Well, it is not the resources that are limited, it is the mindset that we have chosen to be in, is limited. Imagine that if my country grew only potatoes. And since only potatoes are available to me in abundance, will there be any thought of scarcity of wheat or rice in my mind? Absolutely not. I will run happy through the potato fields because all I will know then, will be the great abundance of potatoes in my life. This is a very big problem for the industries that want to grow big in a segment of society that is settled and happy with what they have. In my potato country, the investment of a wheat market will be huge and difficult problem. Before they will be able to sell me wheat, they will have to sell me the need for wheat. And since my happiness will be brimming up by the underground potatoes, creating a space in my happiness for the wheat will be the biggest challenge for any businessman. Why do you think companies spend so much on advertisements while they can easily produce double the amount of their goods and services with that amount? The constant creation of need in the market is the biggest challenge of any business.

Coming back to our dear mosquito. The industry that manufactures mosquito repellants are no different than the wheat or rice or the potato industries. So much so that we do not eat those repellants, but what if I said that you at least breath in those. Well, the companies know that there are side-effects to this kind of usage of insecticides, that we so graciously light up in our bedrooms as we go for a good night's sleep. That is a direct method to slowly kill ourselves. It is just like the chemotherapy. The study says that radiations in chemotherapy kills more of healthy cells than the infected ones. Well, the infected ones too die, but because the number of healthy cells that come in contact with the radiation is higher than the total number of infected cells, the damage of healthy cells is greater. Thus, you know the size of the lungs of a mosquito, and you know the size of your own two. You can do the math out here. Do not bother, I have done it for you. Let's see how big your healthy lungs are compared to an average mosquito. Remember, that includes every single body part of that devil. Consider a mosquito growing to the size of a dog, take a full-grown Labrador, then your lungs will be bigger than a full-fledged football stadium, roughly. One can imagine the damage to the stadium itself if one starts shooting at every place at once to shoot down a goddam bunch of dogs inside the stadium. This is what exactly happens when you put those repellants on and sleep at night. The worst part is that them mosquitos can fly for their lives, but our lungs, our children's lungs suffer with every breath.

So, the next time you light up that mosquito repellant coil, or some fucking fluid for the sake of them mosquitos, do picture Jeff Bezos in front of your good self say, "We change our tools, and then our tools change us."

Chapter 9

IT DEPENDS

While I rubbed my eyes with my fingers, a sense of self love sprung up in to action. I could feel that it was for the first time that I had ever realized my grief in such a deep and sensory way. The touch of my finger-tips became a kind of pleasure and I kept on rubbing my eyes like a child does. I can say that I was weeping and was aware of the fact that I was weeping simultaneously. This is by far the most beautiful feeling of all, in the nature and I had experienced it for the first time in my life. This awareness in turn helped exaggerate the situation. Sometimes, it is good to know that who you are, and what you are into. This helps our brains to produce further questioning of the nature that helps clarify your state. It might feel stupid to question yourself when you are weeping or sad in a sense altogether as a different indifferent being. Somewhat stupid but now I know it was sane to ask questions in that moment. There was this other me who was not troubled by the causes of my misery.

There was a popular advertisement for a watch brand, that aired on the TV when I was in my college and that advertisement really got me thinking. Bollywood star, Aamir Khan, was the brand ambassador of that advertisement. Wearing a different watch every day he says, "I born every day.' It was a captivating slogan. I couldn't imagine how it would be to be born every day back then. Not knowing that years later I would be living the slogan.

By now I was in a state of admiring myself for doing what my parents, friends, family and loved ones have had almost always talked me out from doing. When a child gets hurt, she is encouraged to behave strongly and advised to hide his true feelings for the pain she is feeling. The common notion is that the child cries because she is trying to get attention. True, she is trying to get attention because her understanding of the pain is not as vast as much as her parents' understanding of it is. But if the parents too, have a limited exposure to this emotion, they will not be able to help in that case. Mostly, the parents will either stop the child from crying or give a counselling about how she should have been careful enough. Moreover, a set of rules are then applied in order to prevent such events from cropping up in the near future. What such actions do to the child is sometimes beyond repair. The child is made to believe her reactions to pain are inherently incorrect and that by taking enough caution in future she learns to avoid coming in contact with any kind of pain. We learn early that such a pain not only hurts us, but also makes our loved ones uncomfortable. It is very uncomfortable to be with people who are in pain. We have evolved to seek happiness, and not pain. But little we know that the doorway to happiness is guarded by pain itself.

When I started out with my mission of not killing a single mosquito ever again deliberately, it was reproached by everyone around me. The first people were my immediate family. My spouse went to the extent of asking me if I love her more than the goddam mosquito itself. Now that might seem an exaggeration on her part, but that's what she asked me. My father, from the time I remember, has always professed the idea of sleeping in a mosquito net. Being too lazy, I always refuted his idea. In due course of time, after I got married and became a father, I realized the importance of saving your child from these tiny monsters; the mosquitos. So, at one o'clock in the night, me and my wife were in middle of a very deep discussion inside our mosquito net, while our son was sleeping beside us. While I was talking, she saw a mosquito inside the net. It was just a mild spot on a blue net that my wife managed to see with as little light a room can hold, if the only light is coming from a laptop monitor. Parking our car right on the middle of the highway of the discussion we were on, she entered into a hunter gatherer mode. She asked me to kill it then and there. Since I was too much in the discussion, and I wanted to act and not just talk about moral standards, I told her something that no husband will ever dare to say in situations like these. She was like a lioness asking her lion to get that hyena out of their den. With all due respect to her, I said the most hated word by a wife; No. At first, she thought I was kidding. But when I offered to hold the mosquito in my rounded gapped fist and leave it out of the net, then she was confirmed about my answer. And when I did leave the poor Mrs. Mosquito out of the net, then my wife asked the scariest question, "Do you love the mosquito more than me?".

Well, I believe that if you do such things only to annoy people around you, it can ruin your relationships with them. But if you are sincere and tell them the truth, they will understand and will back you with your idealism. My pain was there, and I cannot be hiding it from the only people I am tied to. Telling or writing about your care for mosquitos, or the tigers, or any of the goddam animals is just a talk or a reading. That love will be true if it is more in your actions than in your words.

Now, when we are stopped and barred to express our own fears and pain, that is inherent to us, in front of those who live amongst us, how can we even start to realize the pain for others. And there is a lot of learning from realizing the pain of others. But to reach there we must start from realizing our own pain. If we know our own pain and fears, and if we dare to address them, at first, we will act immaturely. We will cry, weep, and act in all sorts of ways that are childish. This stage will pass only if we will first enter in this stage. The other stage will be of decision-making. Now, when all the immature ways of calling out to others will start falling and failing, we will enter into a phase, that we can say is an amateur phase. In this phase we will commit a lot of mistakes. But every time we will commit one, the fears and pain will make a record of our own mistakes. This phase too shall pass, but it will pass only if we will deliberately go through this phase. Only if we will commit mistakes on purpose. Unlike the immature phase, this phase will be slow and more intense. The fear of death, that was absent in the immature state, will return to you in this phase. The fear of death is necessary. From the learnings in the immature phase you will learn to use this fear in its most potent ways.

Passing this phase, we come to the most desired and the most awaited stage of all; the mature state. In this state the fruition will take place. This phase is not the ultimate one. There can be any number of phases, but to reach this phase means, there will be no stopping.

At some point all of us want to be young and childlike again. But to the dismay only a handful of us dare to try. You know why? Because of the fear of the pain. But if you commit to yourself that no matter what happens, no matter how dark it gets, I will cross this tunnel and reach the other side of it, and come out as a winner, something very different starts to happen. Something strange and beautiful happens when the youth tries to take a U-turn back to its spoilt sister's place, i.e. adolescence. To the dismay of the youth, he finds his sister is now all grown up. She no more plays the old games she used to. Unable to participate in her new game and too bored to engage in his own, the youth takes its first step toward maturity. This kind of approach to maturity allows a deep retrospection of the adolescence and a practical testing of maturity while you still have time in your youth. But of course, the testing comes with a considerable amount of hit and trial. The most casual attitude will ruin the trip and the highest-level of caution will cancel it entirely. Sometimes you will have to take a trip to both the destinations at least a few couple of times before you can finally make yourself comfortable in the land of the man.

Knowledge or the memory of certain experiences are really specific to the kinds of exposures in that time, we let ourselves open to. Like, only a butcher knows what it is like to chop off the head of a healthy living innocent animal when the butcher knows that his life depends on it. What justification a lawyer can give to himself defending a criminal, he knows has committed the crime, when the lawyer knows his life depends on it. Can anyone measure the sadness of a hangman, when his soul hangs itself every time even before he hangs the convict, when the hangman knows that his life depends on it? Who can stop a man, who carries a hate that measures not in weight but in time, to commit that crime when he knows his life depends on it? No soul is oblivious to its body it carries along, where we see so many bodies that are so oblivious to their own souls that they are very much energized by, and that too, when they know their lives depend on it. Who was I back then? Before this moment, I may not be able to know this ever. It might have been important back then to know, but who am I now is all that matters. And now is the time that I know my life depends on it.